Conversations We Never Had

by

Patrick J. O'Shea (Father)

and

Patrick J. O'Shea (Son)

Copyright © 2008 by Patrick J. O'Shea

ISBN 978-0-7414-5179-8

Published by:

INFI∞ITY
PUBLISHING.COM

1094 New DeHaven Street, Suite 100
West Conshohocken, PA 19428-2713
Info@buybooksontheweb.com
www.buybooksontheweb.com
Toll-free (877) BUY BOOK
Local Phone (610) 941-9999
Fax (610) 941-9959

Published January 2008

Dedicated to my brother,
Ryan Ashley O'Shea,
1975-1977.

I feel like I have denied his existence for thirty years
because it was too hard for me to speak of him.
I'm sorry, my brother.

Patrick and Ryan (1977)

Contents

Foreword and Footnotes

by Carolyn Campbell

Becoming a widow at the age of twenty-five was unexpected and devastating. One of the hardest times of my life was when I had to tell my two young sons, Patrick, age five, and Ryan, age sixteen months, that Daddy was never coming home again. I comforted them and myself with our faith that he is in Heaven and that he felt no pain. He died instantly at the accident scene. It was Patrick's first day of kindergarten.

The next several months were something of a blur. Getting through the holidays with the boys and trying to keep everything "normal" like it used to be was a real challenge. I am extremely grateful for my wonderful parents, Oscar Everett and the late Norma Everett, for all their love and support during this difficult time. My father took over as the boys' father and grandfather and continues to do so to this day. My mother gave me so much love and support and was a wonderful grandmother to my sons. I am extremely thankful to each of them for being such a blessing to our family.

My husband's poetry was such a comfort to me during those lonely times. I am so grateful that he used his God-given talents to communicate his innermost thoughts through poetry. He left a legacy to his family and friends that will live on indefinitely.

Six months after Pat's car accident, my younger son, Ryan, became ill with a stomach virus that was going around. I took him to the doctor on a Friday, and he went into the hospital the same day due to his high fever. He passed away early Sunday morning at the age of twenty-two months. I can't even attempt to describe the devastation and loss I felt. Only a mother who has lost a child can relate to this horror. My main concern was for my son Patrick. He had lost his dad and his only brother in a six-month time frame. I told him that Daddy and Ryan were together in Heaven, and now we had to take care of each other. He is the only thing that held me together for many years. Even to this day, when I feel upset or at loose ends, I call or visit Patrick to feel grounded again.

I am sharing this background information so you can get a better understanding of the basis for this book. This book is about communication. Communication is a vital part of love and life. As I watched my son grow through his teenage years, through college and into a man, my heart aches for his loss. The questions he would have liked to ask his father, the advice he needed from him and the friendship they could be sharing now are all part of the loss he lives with.

The book is laid out in a conversation format. The poems on the left were written by my late husband, Patrick J. O'Shea Jr. (signed: Father), and the poems on the right were written by my son Patrick (signed: Son). Some of the poems written by my son were direct responses to something his dad wrote. Others are poems based on similar thoughts or subjects and were written before this book was conceived.

The poetry his father wrote and Patrick's poetry are a form of communication from the soul. I extend my deepest love and gratitude to my son for all the hours of work he put into this book. His talents are numerous, and

I am sure that his father looks down at him from Heaven with as much pride and love as I have for him.

I am so thankful that my son has stayed strong and made solid choices in his life. Also, I extend tender thanks to his wife, Tracy, for her love and support. They have blessed me with two beautiful grandchildren, Rachael and Shane.

I pray that this book will touch the hearts of all who read it and encourage them to communicate their feelings to their loved ones while they are able to do so.

Thank you again, Patrick, for all your love and support and for giving me a reason to live. This book is a gift of love and something to be very proud of.

Acknowledgements from Patrick J. O'Shea (the father)

THANK YOU*

Thank you
I have no curse
To a friend since birth
I have felt your worth
Though seeing you at worse
I still love you earth
Thank you

Father

* This poem became Pat's epitaph. When I had to choose a memorial stone for him, I wanted it to be unique and personal. Therefore, I used one of his poems. I would like to thank his mother, Esther O'Shea, for helping me with this difficult task. Esther suggested that we put shamrocks on the stone to signify Pat's proud Irish heritage.

Acknowledgements from Patrick J. O'Shea (the son)

Thank you to my dad for leaving volumes of poetry for me to read when I needed it the most. From the way he wrote, I think that he subconsciously knew he would die young and this would be our only connection. Thank you to Oscar Everett, my grandfather, for being a dad to me after my father passed. Thank you also to Norma Everett, my grandmother, for being a second mother. My childhood could have been very bleak, but my mother and grandparents actually made it very good. I ended up with three loving parents! Also, thanks to the rest of the Everett and O'Shea families for their love and support. Several years after my dad and brother passed, I was blessed with a younger sister, Kelly. She helped to fill the emptiness in my life, and we have shared many good times throughout the years. Thank you to my wife, Tracy, for her support and her computer skills, and thank you most of all to my kids, Rachael and Shane. They gave me an overwhelming urge to connect with my dad, and poetry was my only option. Special thanks to Lindy Bowser for the cover illustration. I would also like to thank those who read the drafts of this book and gave me their advice and opinions. You are all appreciated!

TO MY MOTHER

Sometimes I feel like we're in this alone
Why were we left here while they went home
Sometimes in a crowded room
I feel empty and alone
Sometimes I don't know what to believe
And I don't know what to do
I can't comprehend what you went through
I miss my dad
But I cry for you
I miss my brother
But I cry for you

Son

My dad was a Jim Croce fan, as am I. Every time in my life that I heard the song "I Got a Name," one phrase would stick out to me as being very relevant. I did not realize the relevance until I wrote this book!

"I've got a name
And I carry it with me
Like my daddy did
But I'm livin' the dream
That he kept hid" — *Jim Croce*

Day by Day

LEAVING A YOUNG MEMORY*

I remembered the choo-choo train
I imagined in my young mind
Now with suitcase in the morning rain
Riding a railroad, leaving it behind

Father

* Several of Pat's poems refer to trains and the railroad.
During the last five years of his life, he worked for the
railroad at Conway Yards, Pennsylvania. Pat was proud of
his job with the railroad, but he was a poet at heart.

TO DRIVE A CHOO-CHOO

I always wanted to drive a choo-choo
Always wanted to be like you
But the railroad went down the tubes
Guess I'll just write a poem
It's all that I can do
Because what I really wanted
Was to be like you

Son

LIFE OF A WORKINGMAN

Getting up too early, going to bed too late
Is this forever the workingman's fate
Twelve hours a day, seven days a week
I say my patience is at its peak
Where will I find the comfort I seek
The sorry life of a workingman
So tired I can hardly stand
No one's willing to give a hand
Day after day till I kick the can

Father

CAREER VS. JOB

I hang with a surly mob
I have a career
But I don't have a job
Could make more money as an electrician
Could see the light if I were an optician
Could pull some money out of a hat
If I were a magician
But things could be worse
I could be a lying politician
Or a puked-on pediatrician
Money is not all I'm wishin'
So when I'm low on work
I'll just go fishin'
'Tis the life
Of a struggling musician!

Son

THE ENDLESS ROLE

The timeless role
Of a railroad fool
Riding on a train
Outside there's rain
Inside it's plain
Adding his time
Counting the hours
Of a long day
Asking for sunshine
While life slips away
The timeless role
Of a railroad fool

Father

MINGO

The river was brown
The sky was grey
He had money to make
And bills to pay
But there was hope
On this blue-collar workday
When he took a break anyway
And took the time to save
A puppy wandering the tracks
At Mingo Junction

Son

FEED THE MACHINE*

Be a man of strong back and mind
Another skid's coming down the line
Through the dust to be seen
Foreman's coming, gotta feed the machine
Getting sweaty, starting to itch
Gotta roll on this son-of-a-bitch
Ain't got time to build esteem
Foreman's coming, gotta feed the machine
Time gone by, went too slow
Only got five minutes to go
Relieved, leaving showered and clean
Tomorrow again, I'll feed the machine

Father

* Pat wrote this poem while he was working at a local
factory that made ceiling tiles. All day, he fed the tiles into a
machine that cut them into the correct size.

DOWN THE LINE

I've worked some tough jobs in the past
And though those jobs did not last
Physical labor is good for the soul
And I did my best to fit the role
But I could not handle nine to five
Rollin' down the assembly line
Week to week and day to day
Same ol' shit and same low pay
So thank you, dad
For a job well done
Thank you, dad
From a grateful son

Son

NEVER MADE IT AS A STAR

Once one bright and sunny day
Into the golden month of May
I strummed on my string guitar
Though I never made it as a star
I walked alone down to the creek
With a sweet love song to pick
Played a tune on my string guitar
Though I never made it as a star
The birds all gathered at my side
A weeping willow bowed and cried
It must be sad to play a guitar
And never make it as a star
A cow mooed sadly from far away
And the moo just seemed to say
Oh play a tune on your guitar
Though I know you ain't a star
I sang a song that was a sad one
Of a little boy who sang for fun
So long ago with a string guitar
Though I never made it as a star
Animals shed tears when he did play
And they still do to this very day
An old man sits with a string guitar
Though he never made it as a star

Father

BACKSTREET BAR

I love to rock a backstreet bar
I've been playin' music since I was a teen
Jazz, rock, pop and country
And everything in between
I take every chance I get to play
Sometimes workin' without pay
And when I play music
My hands still get clammy
As if I just won a Grammy!
I've played fancy places now and then
But they don't give me that smoky Zen
Of watching the shy get up and dance
With their out-of-shape wives in leather pants
They're all just a little over the hill
But in the moment feelin' that teenage thrill
Though I never made it as a star
I love to rock a backstreet bar

Son

A SONG IS NAUGHT BUT A POEM

I guess I cannot express a feeling in poetry
It's the type of thing not put together
By an alphabet of translated ingenuity
Sing each word dramatically, emotionally
It is no wonder poetry is put to song
I know I cannot write a hundredth poem
That can match a well sung tone
It's hard to inflict the heart the slightest
A mighty phrase may not pierce a soft bone
But they with the power of harmonious voice
Can wrench out your innermost sanctuary of mind
And give much more than words to rejoice
Alas, my poetic mind suffers musical concussions
Each new word is not but a chord progression
A poet of old cries out in regression
"A song is naught but a poem's expression!"

Father

12

SPIRIT OF THE DRUM

It pulses through you
The rhythm feeds life
When the groove is smooth
Everyone feels it right
And if I were the last
Soul on earth
Had nowhere else to run
And no one else to turn to
I would still play the drum

Son

ROCK THE CABOOSE

Don't know if what I hear is true
Grapevines are sometimes old news
They say he drank our wine
Won a grand with just a dime
Shot a guy who couldn't lose
Made a rock & roll band play blues
Streaked as the protesters do

I gotta go, I just got the news
Railroad man, a troublemakin' dude
He's crazy and don't pay no dues
That man don't care, win or lose
Behind the station, without excuse
Me and friends, rock the caboose

Father

TAPS (FOR DRUMLINE)

It's the end of an era
The field is silent now
Under a *Stonehenge* moon
As we make our *separate ways*
Life can be *stone cold*
But *the song remains the same*
We were so tight
Hangin' *late in the evening*
We rocked the "house" on a four-month ride
It makes me believe
The same line will jam again…post game…
On the other side

Son

15

MUSIC

Music is such a wonder
The way it makes one feel
Picking up when under
Making dreams seem real
Playing the melodies sweet
That to us seem dear
In winter or summer's heat
Bring all hearts near

Father

THANK YOU, TO MUSIC

Some voices are high
And some are low
Some a different volume
Some a different tone
Different phonetics
Different shades
But in the end
They're all the same
Dedication, discipline and teamwork
Are a few things I know
Didn't learn them from a book
Learned them from playing a show
And best of all, I'll never be
A corporate clone of society
'Cause music taught me to think
And music taught me to dream
Music lit the way
Through times of darkness
When I might have strayed
So now it's time
That I must say
"Thank You" to music

Son

17

A SIMPLE REVELATION

Running through a field of grass
A gentle wind blows on my face
I wonder at the things that pass
The tears run a face-long race
Gee, it's good to be around
To touch and to be found
Nice to feel a revelation
Fine to have an inspiration

Father

WRITER'S BLOCK

I haven't written in seven long years
I've been sad without tears
I've been mad and drunk beers
It's been seven long years
Life is so crazy
No time to think
Gotta keep movin'
No time for ink
I haven't written in seven long years

Son

POEM TO SHATTER STONE*

Fill me with inspiration
Give me the dedication
With which to write a poem
To weaken hearts of stone
Let it hold the power
Shattering their solid tower
Let it seep into the souls
Of the heart of rock fools

Father

*On several occasions, I tried to convince Pat to get his poetry published. His response made me feel that he didn't think it was the style of poetry people would read. He always added this comment, and though he said it lightly, it made me uncomfortable: "You're never a famous poet until you're dead." My prayer is that this poem, along with the rest of the book, will not only touch but shatter many hearts of stone!

HEART OF ROCK FOOL

For thirty years I carried the weight of stone
But your words of wisdom helped me let go
Sometimes I've confused being cold with being cool
But now I realize I was a heart of rock fool
So I'm writing this to let you know
You wrote a poem that shattered stone

Son

ERIN GO BRAGH

The Irish are some stubborn bulls
A group of fighting, brawling souls
Heavy drinkers are these Micks
Getting drunk they get their kicks
Imagination of a leprechaun
Shamrock luck to rely on
Wondering if there is a green fairy
Of magic tricks and makers of merry

Father

I'M IRISH

I guess I'm Irish
I got it from you!
A temper like a boiling stew
I've been known to be a stubborn ass
I've gotten drunk many times past
But I'm also brave, loyal and true
I guess I'm Irish
I got it from you!

Son

COMBING OUT THE GREY

Comb my hair a hundred ways
Tried to brush out all the grey
Flipped it left, flipped it right
Still I glimpse a sign of white
So I bought some charcoal dye
Thought that would get me by
It looked kinda strange
So I washed the dye out
With a hot water spout
Gonna let the grey be
Don't be like old me
Don't be a dunce
Comb it only once

Father

PUT ON A HAT

In my younger days
I wasted too many hours
Getting too many showers
Combin' my hair in so many ways
To cover the missing and the greys
It's good to be clean
You don't want to stink!
But some days all you need
Is some soap and a sink
So get up and seize the day
Too much vanity is for the weak
Be thankful for what you have
Put on a hat
And just be a dad

Son

VANISHING POINT

Sweaty palms upon the wheel
Eyes fixed on the highway
The smell of burning rubber
A screech as tires go turning
Chrome so brightly flashing
As R.P.M.s are rising
Speedometer has gone berserk
Drops a couple tabs of speed
With a little burst of speed
And as the straightaway ends
Cement roller is in his path
The face is strong and grim
Inside the speed machine
And he is going down
Without slowing down
Died inside the car
No one knew him well
Cops said he was crazy
Hot-rodding to Hell
Or vanishing point

Father

CRUISING THE NIGHT

The T-tops are out
The windows down
95 on the stretch
Warm summer's air whipping through our hair
Cruising the night

Stop for a drink
Flirt with some babes
Forget a new name
Maybe even a number

Back to the car
Crank the starter
Light up the tires
Exit in a cloud of smoke
On the highway
Serpentine through the traffic
Asking for a race
Looking for trouble
Yet always ducking and dodging
'Cause radar pollutes the air
Can't get nailed
Cruising the night

Don't worry 'bout nothin'
Leave your troubles behind
Don't think too much
Just have a good time
Cruising the night

Son

SOMETHING GREATER

Sometimes I think the highway
Is a great conveyor belt
A mass of moving cement
Where the snow don't melt
And something greater says repent
Or accidents will be felt

Father

COFFEE AND TEA

Mr. Coffee and Mrs. Tea
Spent the day Sunday being the best they could be
They talked about love and peace and charity
But on Monday mornin' it was sad to see
Mr. Coffee and Mrs. Tea
Each transformed into an S.O.B. in an S.U.V.
Filled with road rage in the city grid cage
Pullin' out hair in the highway rockin' chair
Flippin' the bird and launchin' the word
It really was sad to see
Mr. Coffee and Mrs. Tea
As teachy and preachy as they could be
Never learned patience or courtesy!

Son

LAUGH AT CLOD

The clod is in every neighborhood
For a laugh he is always good
The same old guy you poke fun at
Calling him dumb, skinny or fat
This, while you tear him apart
Don't you realize, clod has a heart

Father

OLD MAN HAYES

I remember the days
Of an old man named Hayes
Always walkin' every day
They say he's crazy, keep away!
Kids always made fun of him
Sometimes I even joined in
But I knew it was wrong
And my heart felt the sin
I was just a child
Who did not understand
But when I did
I became a man

Son

SANTA CLAUS

You're old enough to understand
Santa is no ordinary man
You can't see the grand ole boy
Who brings the Christmas joy
Santa is a part of men
The goodness of a friend
The meaning behind a gift
A happy spirit in a snow drift
A thought sent from up above
A season for mankind to love

Father

KRISS KRINGLE

When my kids start to doubt
The spirit of old Kriss Kringle
I'll tell them this:
Without him sleigh bells won't jingle
Without him we are in a lonely place
Without him charity has lost its face
Without him the world would feel blue
Without him love won't be true
Without Kriss Kringle
Sleigh bells won't jingle

Son

APARTMENT BOY'S DOG

Oh Mr. Doolittle
Will you whittle
A little dog
From that log
For me

Father

SAFARI

A native hunter told me in a dream
If you look hard enough you'll see
There's a giraffe behind every tree

Son

A BACK WAY HOME

Can't take no more of the city
The air's too thick to breathe
People pushing hot and gritty
Think I'd like to leave
I would even walk alone
If I knew a back way home
An auto horn is blowing
A policeman's whistle too
The noise keeps on going
Fact, I know it's true
I would even walk alone
If I knew a back way home

Father

CHEESE STEAK

Watch the deals go by
As children are hypnotized
By what's cool and what's "phat"
Big business, drug dealers and addicts
Are of the same breed
Sharing the same morals and creed
Selfishness and greed

Get out to change a flat on the expressway
And it might be your final day
'Cause business can't take a five minute delay
So get the hell out of my way!
There's money to be made!

Cities are cities, they're all the same
What really makes me sad is when the sign above
Reads: "Welcome to the city of brotherly love"

Son

JUDGE GOT A HEART

Order! Order!
Roared the Judge
Not a soul did budge
Bring in the suspect, he said
The charge was theft of bread
A district attorney proved his guilt
His own confession was spilt
The Judge asked why he did this thing
The man said his wife was hungering
The Judge said, "No reason to sin"
The man replied, "Rather than starve, I'd do it again"
The jury then did boo and hiss
The Judge just laughed at this
Turned to face the guilty man
To give him a reprimand
The Judge said, "I'll pay for the man's fee"
Then told him he was free

Father

TOO GOOD TO BE TRUE

This story is too good to be true
I wish more people thought like you
A judge with a heart to see the light
A lawyer with the courage to do what is right
A president with a brain to avoid a fight
It's all too good to be true
I wish more people thought like you

Son

BIG MR. POLITICIAN

Big Mr. Politician
Sat in a corner
Counting political gains
Preaching propaganda notes
That came from his throat
Definitely not his brains

Father

POLITICIANS

Some things never change
Politicians lie
Soldiers die
They speak from the throat
Just to get your vote
They tell you what you want to hear
Then forget it all at the end of the year
Politicians lie
Soldiers die
Some things never change

Son

UNEMPLOYMENT LINE

High powers, they can't understand
The unemployed American man
They never stood inside the line
Of malnutrition and epileptic sign
And you know to get the check
Every week, report to misery deck
Why last week, one man's body rung
As someone bumped his iron lung
Even he had to wait his turn
Because the state people are stern
In the idiot line you must stand
To get the money that you demand
Even if you're old and bent
You must stand to pay the rent
Today a man in a wheelchair
Had to stand holding a shoulder there
High powers, they just don't know
Where the unemployed would rather go
The only trouble is called despair
Jobs are scarce everywhere

Father

HEALTH CARE?

A humble custodian turned thirty-eight
Up 'til now his life was great
He worked for peanuts but paid his bills
Thought his policy was good
Until...
He felt a pain in his head
Found a lump that could make him dead
They told his wife and kids not to cry and shout
All we have to do is take it out
We'll get it approved in a couple of days
We'll do the operation and he'll be okay
But just then, Dr. Death swooped in
From a company without a conscience
A company without a sin
Here to bury the hatchet on this poor guy
She opens her shallow briefcase
With only one item inside
A big red stamp
With one word
DENIED

Son

BLEEDER OF THE PEOPLE

Indecisive taxes flog the past
Conflicting ordeals remain unto the last
Governmental powers bleed you every day
Can't anybody find a better way
Be you poor or be you rich
Taxes are a lifetime hitch
No matter where thou may run
Taxes will follow to the sun
Look you up and suck you dry
No logical good reason why
They take the little baby's milk
They take the only thread of silk
Ruin businesses, homes as well
Taxes are a match for Hell
And the story I do tell
May wind up with me in jail

Father

THE WEED

Glanced down at the ground
Saw two flashes of green
Spinnin' all around
Got excited 'bout what I found
A president's head upon the ground
Next to a swirling green oak leaf
Southbound to the ground
So excited and filled with greed
I grabbed at the paper green weed
Changed my mind
And picked up the oak leaf

Son

AGE OF COMPUTERS

A newborn metal race
Taking place of men
They will not get my grace
Nor will I consider them friend
What Simple Simon man
Invented thinking bolts
It's only a tin can
Fed on electric volts
If such a mentality
Could arrange its thoughts
The earth would in fatality
Fall to the rule of robots

Father

AGE OF ROBOTS

They say technology is the way
But jobs get fewer every day
Used to go to the grocery store
And see a smiling face
Now self checkout is the disgrace
Taking the smiling face's place
Even cash has lost its rash
Now plastic is all you need
To send your debt to eternity
The age of robots is upon us
It's just a matter of time
Before the machines start thinking
And leave us all behind

Son

QUIET MOMENTS

Lingering, lounging quiet moments at home
Peace of mind, thoughts are so kind
A place of places we have known
When a need of rest is shown
A calmness at a time of need
An escape from society's seed
Just the same, you got to roam
To enjoy the quiet moments at home

Father

THE LUNATIC AND THE CLOCK

You may think I'm a lunatic
But I like to hear the clock tick

Technology has gone berserk, you see
Computers, video games, and Hi-Def T.V.
If I want to watch reality
I'll hang a mirror and just watch me!

I hope the power is out tonight
And I see my wife in candlelight
I hope it's out tomorrow too
Maybe I'll take the kids to the zoo

I really have all I need
Maybe I'll pick up a book and read
Or write a letter to an old friend
Just to remind him friends don't end

You may think I'm a lunatic
But I like to hear the clock tick

Son

WATER THAT A ROCK WON'T SKIP

Hey there, my little friend
Will you lead me to the river?
I have a dime and time to spend
And I am not an Indian giver
I once lived in this here town
I no longer know my way around

Sir, the river is now a spoil
The fish do naught but toil
In a red river of cattle slaughter
Along with wreckage in the water
My eyes can't penetrate the bottom
No matter how hard I concentrate
Vision can't infiltrate the scum

Well, my friend, you changed my trip
It would be suicide to take a dip
In water that a rock won't skip
Although I told you once before
I'd give a dime for a chore
I changed my mind about the price
Decided a quarter, for good advice

Father

THE DEVIL JUST LAUGHS

I once lived near a factory
All the trees were dead downwind
All the animals ran and hid
All the fish jumped out of the river
'Cause the scum they dumped
Could make catfish quiver
'Round midnight
They would blow cancer out of the stacks
For all of us peasants to breathe
Sometimes they would get caught
And pay a fine, or so we thought
But they had enough money to do it again
And the devil just laughs
Watching us choke
On our own damn sin

Son

WALK IN THE PARK

Feeling tired and beat
Mind in aggravation
Temper all in heat
Try some relaxation
Go out at dark
Take a walk in the park
Trouble's on its way
Strain's too much to hide
Hurry, don't waste a day
Release what's inside
Go out at dark
Take a walk in the park
Listen all my friends
Enemies just the same
Life has many bends
Try to keep feelings tame
Go out at dark
Take a walk in the park

Father

WALK IN THE WOODS

Take a walk in the woods
Take your kids
Take your dog
Take a snack
Sit on a log
Leave your troubles
Leave your worries
Leave now
But do not hurry
Life's too fast
Life's too crazy
Take time to relax
It's not being lazy
It'll make you feel good
Take the time
Take a walk in the woods

Son

LUCKY RABBIT'S FOOT

Silence cracked and thunder roared
Steel balls rained from the sky
The ground was red with blood
There was thunder then the cry
My son lay dead in the mud
Fear overcame me at the scent of man
Hunter and killer of my helpless son
In a bound I jumped and ran
Heard the thunder of the gun
My memory will soon be put
On a chain, the lucky rabbit's foot

Father

NO EVIL BOLL WEEVIL

I'm a fisherman just like you
But I have become a hunter too
Hunting has taught me conservation
Respecting wildlife and preservation
I know there are some men of evil
Poaching and killing, they're evil boll weevil
But I am not of this sort
So, I'll promise you this
Or how should it be put
I'll never kill a rabbit
Just for its foot.

Son

THE ELEPHANT WHO THOUGHT

I am the elephant
Who was bitten by a bee
Who giggled at the monkey
Laughing, loving to laugh
At the silly, sulky giraffe
Though to people I am shy
Staring people make me cry
Peek-a-boo, they can't see me
I'm hiding behind a bamboo tree
Ouch! That darn old bee

Father

I USED TO LOVE THE ZOO

I saw a giraffe at the city zoo
I told my daughter, "He looked at me and you!"
And with his eyes he asked us
"Is there anything you two can do?"
The trees were all covered with wire
Crushing his every desire
His cage was a cement can
He lived like a criminal man
If I worked here I'd break him out
If I could I'd build an ark
And float him out after dark
I'd set them all free
Two by two
Cause I wouldn't have the heart
To work at the zoo!

Son

DOWN AT RIVER PIER

Things look bad in town
So I come down here
If you're looking 'round
I'm down at river pier

Really not a river
Really not a pier
Only a small stream
A boat dock log
It takes the place
Of city fog

I'm a man
You understand
When I see things
Looking out of hand
I go where silence rings
Down at river pier

If up there, I ain't found
Look down the hillside
You'll see me hang around
The sandy waterside
'Cause them blues I steer
I'm down at river pier

Father

CAMPFIRE

There's something about a campfire
I just can't explain
I could watch for hours
And not have to strain

There's something about a campfire
Helps me drift away
The smoke fills my mind
With the good ole days

There's something about a campfire
That makes us understand
There's something spiritual
That's been given to man

Son

I'M GONNA BUILD ME A CASTLE

In my mind
I'm gonna build me a castle
In some unknown faraway land
No one there to wreck or hassle
My mental fortress of golden sand

In my mind
I'm gonna build it by a wavy sea
And if I should feel lonely
I may invite a friend for tea
It's gonna be a fine place to see

In my mind
I'm gonna build me a castle
Better than the best I've known
I'd let you come if I could
It's only a vision I have shown
It's in my mind

Father

I'M GONNA BUILD ME A CABIN

In my mind
I'm gonna build me a cabin
Way back in the woods
Where the busses don't run
And the air is still good

In my mind
The cabin is near a lake
Fed by clear mountain streams
Filled with brook trout
And lined with hemlock trees

In my mind
I am not alone
My best friend is a dog
And this cabin I call home
Me, the cabin, the dog and God
This vision is my own

Son

I CAME UPON A TOAD

As I was walking a country road
I came upon an ugly toad
He looked up at me in fright
Then hopped right outta sight
It just goes to show
How much we humans know
For the ugliness I saw in he
I think he saw in me
Or did I step on him?

Father

COMPELLED

I saw a butterfly on the sidewalk
With a broken wing
He knew he was sure to die
As did I
I was compelled to place him
In the grass and say goodbye
I don't know if anyone cares
Or if it matters
Or why
But it just felt right

Son

IT

It warms our hearts so well
It opens our minds so much
It you cannot really sell
It you cannot really touch
It is an easy thing to do
It sometimes lingers awhile
It, my friend, is a smile

Father

POWER OF A SMILE

When you live as close to the city as I
People get caught up in time
They forget common courtesy
They forget to smile!
So think on it if you would
Think about it a long, long while
And don't underestimate
The power of a smile!

Son

RATHER BE YOU

See a rich man on the street
Hope for the treasure at his feet
You don't want to take his place
You want the riches, not his face
So all in all, yes it is true
You would rather be you

See a fish swim in the sea
Wish you could be so free
You don't want no scaly gills
Ugly fish fins give you chills
So more and more you find
You'd rather be with your own kind

See anybody that is anywhere
Think that you might be there
You just don't wanna be he
The part is not really me
So on and on it seems known
The best life is your own

Father

JUST TO BE YOU

To make your own way
Is hard to do today
To speak the truth
Seems so uncouth
To do what's right
Takes a fight
To just be you
Is hard to do
So do what you can
To be a good man
Do whatcha need to do
But whatever that is
Just be you

Son

FEAR OF GROWING OLD

Once, looking in a lily pond
I saw reflections to think upon
In the still water of images
I saw myself in later ages
Wrinkled, worn, out of tune
A face that aged too soon
Some wrinkles indicated happiness
Others showed much sadness
Though I know the image will fade
Of oldness, I am afraid

Father

THE PRICE I PAY

Growing older can actually be fun
I'm older than you, though I'm your son
Sometimes I feel like I'm fallin' apart
But I've learned to live more from the heart
I learn new things every day
And wisdom is worth the price I pay
Hope I live to be old and grey
'Cause wisdom is worth the price I pay

Son

MYSELF

Living with
Living without
Living only
With myself

Doing things
Doing not
Doing nothing
With myself

No understanding
No unknowing
No underestimating
With myself

Being so
Being no
Can show
I don't know
Myself

Father

OPEN AIR

Step outside
Breathe and look around
You can't be afraid
Take the time
Step outside your walls
And look inside
If you don't take the time
You could end up losing your soul
And probably losing your mind

There's a lot more to ourselves
Than our illusions tell us
Some are trying to get to Heaven
By saying "the hell with everyone else"
Others lock into a groove
That's too square to break out of
So find it in yourself
A place where love and freedom thrive
You can't be afraid
Take the time
And step outside.

Son

A WOMAN

A woman is so thrilling
With all the extra feeling
The hardships that she bears
Show she really cares
A woman is so tender
Thoughtful tears and such
Love's own true contender
A loving woman's touch

Father

INTO THE SUN

I sailed my ship into the sun
On the way
I met an angel and a nun
The angel smiled and said, "Hi!"
The nun smiled and said, "Goodbye"
And when my work here is done
At least I can say
I met an angel and a nun

Son

EVERYBODY'S LOOKING

Everybody's looking for a rainbow
Their eyes are searching upward
It's sad that they don't know
The rainbow is found below

Everybody's looking for pots of gold
Their eyes are ever peering downward
I really believe they should be told
Riches are found in what hearts hold

Everybody's trying for an easy way
Their eyes are ever peering savagely
I think maybe someone should say
Life is lived, day by day

Father

JUST A THOUGHT

Sometimes your mind spins 'round
Lookin' forward then lookin' back
At what will and couldn't last
You can remember
But never dwell
On hardships and losses
Felt in the past
Then again, don't look too hard for tomorrow
You might miss today
And it could be your last

Son

WILL YOU MAYBE

Never been a churchgoing man
Never much of a religious hand
Only said a prayer or two
But I believed in you
So if you don't take me
Please, take my wife and baby

Father

SUNDAY MORNIN' MAN

He cuts deals all week long
Beats his kids when they are wrong
Makes his wife live in fear
Brags of the money he makes each year
But on Sunday mornin'
He puts on his best suit and tie
To further his lifetime lie
Puts on a Sunday mornin' show
His attendance is stellar
But his heart doesn't go
He'll smile at you and shake your hand
He's the Sunday mornin' man

Son

Facing Clouds

MY LITTLE SON*

Laugh and giggle my little son
It feels good to know you're having fun
Your smile is like the powerful sun
Play with your toys and when you're done
Go to sleep, my little son

Father

* This poem became Ryan's epitaph. His memorial stone is designed like his father's but with a different poem and a small lamb carved on the top of the stone.

SIMPLE JOY

Sittin' in a beanbag chair
With my son
Doesn't matter what I have
And haven't done
In this moment
This is this
I'm his father
He's my son

Son

A CHILD — STANDING PROUD

He is just a child
Who is standing proud
Do not boo nor laugh
He is just a child
Who is standing proud

If in a ballgame he does strike out
Hold back a shout
He is just a child
Who is standing proud

Problems can be tough
This you must know
So if a little head
Is hanging too low
Tell him to stand proud
He is just a child

Father

FAITH OF A CHILD

In our younger days
My sister and I were not close in age
Sometimes I felt like I was her father
Sometimes a brother not to be bothered
One day she kept bugging me to go fishin'
In a small stream way back in the woods
But I kept tellin' her this:
"The stream is too small! No fish! No good!"
But when I saw the disappointment she had
I stopped being a brother, and tried to be a dad
We took a half-mile hike in the summer heat
And before I could coach her or even find a seat
She threw her line in
With a little sister grin
And caught a trout, shiny and clean
Prettiest fish two kids ever seen
I couldn't believe it!
For on that day a girl got her wish
And the faith of a child
Had caught her a fish!

Son

ANGRY CHILD

No, can't go, little boy
So play with some toy
It don't look like rain
So don't you complain
You say you are mad
You say you are sad
Tell me, whatcha gonna do
If we go to the zoo
And a tiger escapes
Comes after you!

Father

TERRIBLE TWOS

The terrible twos
Give parents the blues
The guardian angel needs a rest
The devil jumps in to do his best
Seethin' and teethin'
A miserable heathen
It will fade in a couple of years
It will wash away with a couple of beers
It will make you ask, "what did I do?"
When your cute little baby
Turns the terrible two!

Son

ONLY ONE

There were pretty faces in my past
Loves that never seem to last
Thus, I knew I found the one
And I'll be darned...A son!

Father

RACHAEL E.

Rachael E., I love thee
And I love your mother so much more
Since you were sent by the Lord
You brought a new light to my world
I've never seen such a beautiful girl
When in life you face fear
Never forget that daddy's here
When I have to set you free
Remember these words from me
Rachael E., I love thee

Son

OUR NEWBORN SON

He brought a new joy to our life
It was not there before
He gave a happiness to my wife
More than she could wish for
He gave us new hopes and plans
For the many years to come
As he reaches out his little hands
We give thanks for our newborn son

Father

MY SON

The Lord has given me a gift
That I can only repay
With my very own soul
A gift greater than fame, power or gold
He has given me a namesake
To carry on when my time is done
He has blessed my life
And has given me a son

Son

HAPPY LITTLE CHAINS

He wakes up with a cry
Does he feel alone
We think we really try
To make ours a loving home
He hugs us with a smile
Upon his little face
Feeling all the while
His need for our embrace
We wonder what he's thinking
As he plays his little games
We hope his thoughts are linking
Into happy little chains

Father

A DRIFTING BALLOON

Children grow up too soon
Like the sadness of a drifting balloon
Memories heard in the call of a loon
Forgetting the wonder of the moon
Rainbows and sunsets will fade away
Clouds will cover a sunny day
All the colors will turn to grey
When kids learn about man's way
Children grow up too soon
Like the sadness of a drifting balloon

Son

THE BABY SWING

Oh little baby
Laughing on a swing
Mom is standing by
With a song to sing

Father

YOUNG SPIRIT

My unborn child
Knows more than I
Yet, I have the
Awesome responsibility of teaching him!

Son

MY LITTLE CHILD

My greatest prize, my only son
I am young, you are so young
It grieves me when you're down
It hurts to see you out of fun
Tonight I cry for you
Don't wanna see ya' lonely, boy

My little child, my only son
You make me laugh and smile
Don't pass the happy hours
I worry all the while
Don't wanna see ya' lonely, boy

My truest heart, my little son
You really are so young
I feel a small rain cloud
Inside your precious little soul
If your head is low and hung
Don't wanna see ya' lonely, boy

My flesh, my only son
I hear you call me daddy
I'm old, young, not so young
I hope you will be happy
Don't wanna see ya' lonely, boy

Father

DREAM OF MY FATHER

I woke up and saw him standing there
Surrounded by a snowstorm
Dressed in black with a 1969 hippy's hat
Was I dead or just dreaming
Immortal idol standing before me
I couldn't speak my will
'Cause his soul was too clean
He looked at me and smiled
The tears froze in my eyes
He told me to hold on to my dream
A spirit never lies
A snowflake is a unique masterpiece
Of the Lord
That doesn't stay too long

Son

THE HEART THAT'S TRUE

It's hard to live this life I live
To love, be loved and wanting love
It's hard to say, a heart for a heart
When you feel things fall apart
It's hard sometimes, still you do
Love the heart that's true to you

Father

VALENTINE

Follow your heart
It might take time
But it'll get you there
To a state of love
So don't be scared
Follow your heart

Son

FREE ME, LOVE ME

Free me from the chains
Which hold us far apart
Love me and erase the stains
Which have broken our hearts

Free me from the reins
Unexisting at the start
Love me when it rains
Teardrops are a work of art

Father

THE TRUTH

I'm through holding my feelings in
For the sake of others
For the sake of sin
I care for you deep in my heart
A deeper friendship I'm willing to start
My love for you I just can't hide
I'm tired of holding my feelings inside
I love you!

Son

MY LOVE

Touch my hand……my love
Help me stand……..my love
In this land………..my love
Plays a band……….my love
For us……………...my love

Father

WITH LOVE

Open your heart and let me in
Feel the love in the touch of my hand
I thought falling in love was such a sin
You stole the love out of my soul
Our heated passion will never go cold
I'm falling in love with you
You mean so much
You held on when I was down
And brought my feelings back in touch
With love

Son

TELL ME, MY LOVE

Tell me, my love
Will you love me when I am old
To always treat me good as gold
Let me know I'm not being fooled
For I fear your heart turning cold

Tell me, my love
Will you love me with tender care
To never use my heart to tear
Stand beside me through my despair
When the hurt's too hard to bear

Tell me, my love
Will you love me when I am grey
To treat me affectionately in every way
Yet never tire of me each passing day
No longer will I be young and gay

Tell me, my love
Will you love me when I'm not strong
I'll need you most to get along
Believe I love you too, forever long
Your smile itself fills me with a song

Father

I KNOW IT

Lately,
Love has been hard to feel
And harder to show it
But in my heart
I know it
You're the one for me
Our kids, our souls
Eternity

So,
It's been hard to feel
And harder to show it
But in my heart
I know it

Son

IF I HAD WINGS

If I had wings
I'd be flying to you
It's one of those things
That can't come true
But you can tell everybody
This is our poem
It's not for anybody
It's just our own
You can tell by this note
What I'm thinking of
It's in what I wrote
To you my sweet love
Yes, if I had wings
I'd be flying to you
Please don't you cry
And this is why
You can tell everybody
This is our poem
It's just our own

Father

LONG DISTANCE

Each day we're apart seems longer
But don't lose faith
'Cause my love for you grows stronger
Every time you think I'm not missing you
I'm actually wishing I was kissing you
And every time you think we're growing apart
I'm actually loving you more from the heart
So don't worry, little one
The distance between us is only land
And my love for you is greater
Than the earth's every grain of sand

Son

FACING CLOUDS

Can't give you much in money
Hardly a single dime
Still days may be sunny
Place your hands in mine

Days may be getting longer
It will take some time
Making our love grow stronger
Unless you leave me behind

Let's go searching together
For a way through wilds
Stay with me forever
It's easy to face clouds

Father

WHITE PICKET FENCES

I remember when we'd cruise through town
With the windows down
Yellin' and laughin' and singin' out loud
Sometimes I'd dream too much
But you never put me down
We lived for love
And hoped someday we'd have

White picket fences
A nice green yard
White picket fences
A two-car garage
White picket fences
Small town dreams
White picket fences
Just you and me

Son

WE ARE ONE

You are my blood
Racing into my heart
And I would not be
If we were to part

You are my skin
Protecting my soul
Without you I'd freeze
The air is so cool

You are my mind
Making up my ways
And if pain strikes you
In me the pain stays

You are my love
My reason for life
You are the one
You are my wife

Father

MIRRORS OF THE SOUL

Two mirrors standing face to face
Seeing themselves forever in each other
A mutual view that lasts to eternity
It's hard to find
Two mirrors in that place
Reflecting their love
Finding truth in the other's face
When I look into the eyes of my wife
I realize
I have become
One of those two mirrors
Standing face to face

Son

LOVE AND THE SEA

Our love is like the sea
Turbulence and destiny
Quakes, whitecaps of raging waves
Rising tides and barren bays
Misty mornings ever endlessly
The shores forever defensively
Wind with wet blown sprays
Sunlight's soothing warm rays
It's like the love we know
On and on it will flow

Father

PLAYGROUND

Our love is like a seesaw
Sometimes high
Sometimes low
Changes like the weather
But I know
It's balanced in our hearts

Son

Lifetime Pain

LIFE'S NOT LIKE THESE FAIRYTALES*

Before you go to bed
Take a word of advice, my son
Listen to me well
You will learn in days to come
Life's not like these fairytales

Hey, my little man
Understand as you grow older
These things I can't foretell
Go ahead, cry on daddy's shoulder
Life's not like these fairytales

Oh, tiny little young one
Get wise to the world of man
Know what you buy or sell
Make it the best you can
Life's not like these fairytales

As you fall asleep
Remember mistakes you make
Try harder when you fail
Love only when there's love to take
Life's not like these fairytales

Father

* This poem was read at Pat's funeral. Many of his friends
and coworkers had no idea that he wrote poetry. I believe
that somewhere in his soul, he knew he would die young.
Everyone was touched deeply by this poem.

FAIRYTALES

I learned this lesson
When I was five
When they told me
You were not alive
And when my brother
Left me too
Then and there
I knew
These fairytales
Are untrue

Son

MY BOY

My boy
My boy
My pride
My joy
I'll love you
When I go
I'll love you
When I go

Father

IF ONLY I COULD

You left me at an early age
But I know it wasn't by your will
Didn't have a chance to teach me much
But what you taught me, you taught me well

I wear your cross every day
And your memory I will always save
My eyes turn glossy and tears they fall
Every time I visit your grave

Dad, I respect you
And hope someday I'll be as good
Wish I could see you again
I'd tell you I love you, if only I could

Son

MY BROTHER

I never bowed my head in shame
By letting my brother hold the blame
If a friend or anyone other
Ever talked ill against my brother
I wouldn't let it go unheard
I wouldn't fight or say a word
I'd walk away from my old friend
And he'd know it was the end
Because no friend is worth a brother

Father

THE CONVERSATION

Hello, my brother
It's been a long time
Since I stopped by
To wish you a Merry Christmas
And to let you know
How life is back home

Mother is doing ok
She got a new job
With a slight raise in pay
She still thinks about you
And hopes to see you again someday
Life has been hard on her
And through it all she's been strong
But when you look in her eyes
You can still see the pain

You have a younger sister
That you never got to know
She's in high school now
And sixteen years old
She plays clarinet and a baton she twirls
She's a very talented
And beautiful young girl

As for me,
I'm twenty-five and getting married in June
I wish you could be my best man and meet my wife
But I can't get a hold of you
By mail or by phone
All I can do is talk…
To this cold lonely stone

Son

MISSING MEMORIES*

I miss the ragged, shaggy dog named Boots
He used to run happily at my side
Our friendship was the deepest roots
Then one day not long away Boots died
Now only a memory lingers hither
And I miss the lazy moving river
I miss the things I should have done
When I was small, carefree and young
I can even remember the days of fun
With a Popsicle pressed to my tongue
Now time's become an Indian giver
And I miss the lazy moving river
I miss the friends I have once had
It was long ago on the waterside
We used to swim so free and glad
Now it's gone in a forgotten tide

Father

* Shortly after Pat's death, Boots was found wandering the
cemetery where Pat's body was laid to rest. Nobody could
understand how the dog managed to get there. There was a
river to cross as well as many busy roads and bridges.

MY SHADOW

I lost my shadow
It was just here!
But clouds rolled in
It's gone, I fear!

It would follow me everywhere
Out to the shed or to the back yard
Out to the driveway to jump in the car
Walks in the park and walks in the woods
I loved my shadow like no one could

Now she's gone to be with God
And since my brother never had a dog
I hope that they can be together
Running and playing, light as a feather
Jumping from cloud to cloud
Barkin' and laughin' out loud
Happy as happy can go
But I still miss my shadow

Son

INTOXICATED MEMORY

I was high
Yet could not forget
A love gone by
So still I wept

Father

HEART BREAK

Tears drip from the eyes of a wounded soul
Like blood from a heart
With a wooden stake, called love
Driven through it

Son

NO LAUGHING BREEZE

Laughingly the breeze danced around the trees
Crystal minnows frolicked amidst blue seas
Trumpets blasted clouds with sweet love
Sunlight split splendor on the wings of a dove
Majestic stallion galloped the fields in glee
These things were nice to feel and see
Yet this lonely lost heart knows misery
The one I love has set me free
And the tree feels no laughing breeze

Father

WILL THE SUN RISE?

The sun sets softly
With a red mist and a purple haze
The evening star is in the sky
But the shadow of darkness is rollin' in

The sun might not rise tomorrow
But then again it might
True love won't wait for tomorrow
It's calling your name tonight

I heard the lonely whistle
Of a southbound midnight train
My memory is still with you
And my heart can't take the pain

Standing on the highest mountaintop
In the dark before dawn
Free spirit in search of an angel
Hoping for your light to come my way
Rediscover our love and dawn a new day

Son

DIRTY SHAME

I was just a young man
When I saw your face
And if you'd have run
I would have given chase
It seems like yesterday
Words of ice, lips of fire
Yes, it hurts to go away
But hearts don't stand on wire
It's not strange to be in pain
Me and you have been through this
A shelter doesn't stop the rain
So cold we came together
Warming ourselves for awhile
It's a shame it wasn't forever
A dirty shame we can't smile
Many times we laughed and cried
And I am sorry to see it end
Yet, I won't take no fool's ride
It's all right but I lost a friend

Father

RED ELK PARK

Red Elk Park, after dark
There's a spider on the swing
Thought we knew everything
But in the end
I lost a friend
Now here I sit
In Red Elk Park, after dark
Alone

Son

MYSTIFIED

I know you lied
I'm mystified
I have tried
Also cried
I'm mystified
Saw you in town
Takin' a ride
With another man
I'm hurt inside
Can't understand
I'm mystified
Tell me, girl
Open wide
Thought you a pearl
I was wrong
I'm mystified

Father

DISBELIEF

Ain't easy to open your heart again
After you've cried your last tear
Ain't easy to love again
When your love becomes your past
Just when you think you found true love
She has no mercy on your heart
I give up on love
It ain't worth a damn
Don't want no woman bringin' me down
Rock-n-roll will be my last stand
Why believe in love?
Sometimes I don't even know if it exists
Just when you think your dream girl loves you
She gives you a good-bye kiss
They say a man learns from his mistakes
Yet one I consistently seem to make
Love is a power way too great
To resist

Son

ALCOHOLIC'S THOUGHT

What would happen if my libido was lost
Could I still dream or hope for more
No — I doubt it — the Devil names the cost
The price is much deeper than my soul
For the brandy once burst into flames
Dazed, I retrospected a part of my past
So forth it came, a rush into my veins
Oh, I cried, the cry that was my last
In the last moment I was without wealth
And I knew I had destroyed myself

Father

ALCOHOLIC'S WIFE

She makes his coffee
Yet she doesn't know why
And when the sun sets
In the evening sky
She tries not to cry
She decorates the tree
Humming Silent Night

Son

DESPAIR

The rain came down
On my head
I said, "Stop!"
Tears I shed
Said, "Rain, rain go away
Come again some other day"
Don't need the rain
Don't need the pain
"Go away!" I said
The rain came down
On my head
Tears wet the pillow
On my bed

Father

THE PAIN I FEEL INSIDE

I believe love can ever last
And should not be blocked by walls of the past
I've made mistakes, this I know
But you've changed my life
And I won't let go
You mean more to me
Than you'll ever know
Sadness, regret and emotions flow
You might not see me cry
I'm controlled by my pride
But I can't explain
The pain I feel inside
Forgive me

Son

FORGIVE ME

Oh Lord
Forgive me
Losing faith
Unbelieving thee
Oh Lord
My God
I do worship
Thee God
Oh Lord
Of Heaven
Hell and Earth
Forgive one
Wrong since birth

Father

REGRET

Help me, Lord
My blood, it boils
This fire is getting hotter
The chains of sin
Drag me down
Drag me down
Deep into death
Regretting my actions
For resurrection I pray
'Cause this world is a prison
My soul, it needs to be saved
I wish that in life
I would've changed my ways
Now it's too late…
Hell is my grave

Son

GOD'S WAY

The world will turn and cities will burn
Mothers will cry and soldiers will die
The thieves will steal and killers kill
That's just the way it is today

The world will turn and stars will burn
The birds will sing and church bells ring
The children will play and all will be gay
That's just the way it is today

The world will turn and we shall learn
The peace of love and better times
What life is of and a dividing line
Things are not what they should be
God is on his way, it must be God's way

Father

GOD'S PUZZLE

Each day we build a new piece
The picture starts to get clearer
And the end starts to get nearer
Some days may feel like a total waste
But do not accuse anyone in haste
Some days the piece you build is not for yourself
Some days you build a piece for someone else
We are all too young to understand
The complexities of the master plan
I will not lie to you, my friend
When you finish your puzzle, it will be the end

Son

THE RAIN AND LONESOME PAIN

I woke up early in the morning
Looked out just to see it raining
It seemed to be a day of mourning
And this young heart's complaining

I woke up alone, under cold sheets
Looked out just to see no sunshine
All I saw was the same old streets
All I wanted was to feel fine

I woke up early to shed some tears
Looked outside just to see the rain
All I felt was the same old fears
It was the rain and lonesome pain

Father

I CAN'T COMPLAIN

I've felt the rain and lonesome pain
I've asked God to take my hand
And take me from this land
But my work here is not done
Now I have a daughter and a son
A new purpose, a new love
And when it pours from up above
I need to be strong
And not complain
About the rain and lonesome pain

Son

NOTHING

Nothing is the pause of a heartbeat
A momentary suspension of the time
The gap between a comet and its fire
What's betwixt you and the cold sheets
Elapsed time from high speed to stop
The silence after the wolf call

Father

PRESENCE

Let me tell you about this sound I've heard
You won't understand by listening to me
Because it can't be explained by words
You have to step outside
Alone
Just after a deep snow
And breathe the cold winter air
Be still and listen
The sound will be there
I'm not asking you to understand my patience
Nor to feel my pain
Just to listen to this sound
It's very soft, yet you don't have to strain
You can't hear it with your ears
So don't even try
It's only heard from the soul
I know it's there
But I'm not sure why

Son

PARANOID

Somebody's watching me
Someone hovering at my back
Eyes look down from every tree
Think they wrote my name in black
And being paranoid is easy

Racing in my car
Think the law's on the next street
In my mind sirens blow from afar
Lights flashing by, an entire police fleet
Paranoid, I sit in my seat

I know someone's close behind
I hear the tapping of their shoes
Maybe it is just in my mind
I get the bloodhound hunter blues
I find I'm paranoid

Father

TIRED MIND

Lying in bed
Covered by darkness
Surrounded by silence
Alone
Lack of sound feels almost safe
But nothingness has intensity
Especially if you wait
If you listen too hard
You just might hear
Soft squeaky footsteps
Of a shadow with a knife
Sneaking up your stairs
Then again, you're probably just
Paranoid, tired and scared
So save your mind
Get some sleep

Son

AWAITING GRANDPA

Old man walking down the street alone
Hard day's work and heading home
Can't wait to see sweet grandma
Hear the children say grandpa
Only walking, thinking, old eyes blinking
Carries a present for Johnny
And a red balloon for Tommy
The old guy wouldn't hoard a dime
To take away a kid's good time
Good times, they sometimes end
The two little kids await a friend
Turn a corner, a block to go
A smile showed, he did not know
Two cruel thugs planned a roll
On this happy old loving soul
They waited for his coming
One impatient, the other humming
The music stopped, the old man came
Two thugs now share the blame
Knocked an old man down
Put him deep in the ground
Two small kids cry on a shoulder
Two thugs rummage through a folder
A police car comes, blows a tire
A voice said, "Halt or I will fire"
Thugs ran and lost their lids
Awaiting grandpa is two small kids

Father

ANDREW, THE PIANO MAN

He was a big fat piano man
From some town up north
Came to Nashville to make a stand
To see what he was worth
We tried to help, let him join our band
But his hands were too fat and his fingers too slow
He knew…we knew…we had to let him go

A few days later, I saw him sittin' by the old tracks
Waitin' to hop a train
I said, "ain't been a train here in years"
Just then we heard a whistle blow
Andrew said, "it's time to go!"
He climbed a rock and jumped atop
A rusty old train
The train went faster and faster
Then he saw lights, cameras and actors
And people screaming about a disaster
Then he realized the train he hopped atop
Was a rusty old prop
Headed for a two-hundred-foot drop
No time to jump
No time to yell
The train plowed through a barrier
And plunged towards hell!

Son

DEATH OF A CHIEF

The chief looked to the sea with hate
At the ship which would be his fate
The sky was dark, the hour late
As the captain came ashore with his mate
The chief was promised goods and treats
Ha! He didn't know that pirates cheat
It took ten men to make his defeat
They bound him at his hands and feet
On the Devil his capture he blamed
As he tugged at stakes holding him chained
With the struggle his strength he had drained
Still he was not to be tamed
Despite the looks he gave the pirate crew
Their crazy ways and alcoholic brew
In this place, other bones did strew
Now the chiefs would be amongst them too
The cannibal died like a dog

Father

ARROW TRUTH

I am an Indian
Drawing a bow
Don't cross me
Or I might let go
You pissed in my rivers
You butchered my trees
You raped my land
Now let me be!
I lived with the buffalo
The moon and the sun
But you wrecked it all
With greed and a gun
Now leave this land
You human disease
And don't come back
Please, Please, Please!

Son

A PRANKSTER LAUGHS IN SILENCE

The phone call came at eight o'clock
It gave the school quite a shock
Someone said, "a minute to evacuate
A second behind is way too late"
A bomb threat at the public school
Firemen came with the detecting tool
No bomb was located, nothing was found
No explosion broke into the sound
A prankster laughs in silence
Idiotically at his defiance
Okay, the prankster got a grudge
Against a big wheel in the fudge
But what gives him a right to judge
Who should suffer, who should pay
Only children losing a school day
Does he care as he laughs away?

Father

I HOPE AND PRAY

You won't believe this
But bomb threats are old school
Now school shootings are cool!
What happened to karma
And the golden rule?
Politicians blame the guns
But I blame the breakdown
Of fathers and sons
Family values are fading away
No time for fishin'
Gotta work harder and get more pay
The world is getting pretty scary
Think we all need to sit down
And watch Little House on the Prairie
Can't teach morals in school anymore
And Heaven forbid you sing Silent Night
It just ain't right!
These days, people just want to kill and fight
I hope someday we see the light!
I pray someday we see the light!

Son

DEATH OF THE WARRIOR WAR

There was a man named War
Who rode a majestic white horse
Clad in forgotten armor of Thor
Like an Olympic God of War
He is there when a soldier dies
Though he's only a dream of course
I can see tiredness of hearing cries
I see sadness in the glint of his eyes
I watched his flowing hair turn grey
I could see War had lost its source
He dropped the sword, tossed the shield away
War had fought his last war this day
War's jaws were set in a grim line
Suddenly they broke into a smile
His horse began to wobble with time
And then both were but a dust pile
I only wish the dream was true
For everyone, for me and for you
Make peace your newest cry
Hope for the death of the Warrior War
Hope that war does surely die
What wish could mean more?

Father

WAR WILL NEVER DIE

After thousands of years
And billions of tears
We have not evolved
Past a caveman's mind
And war will never die
No matter how many mothers cry
Politicians will lie
The eagle will fly
Everyone is teaching and preaching
About love and peace
But oil prices are just too sweet
Greed can't resist a tempting treat
So mothers and fathers say goodbye
Sisters and brothers say goodbye
Because war will never die
Why can't we learn?
Why? Why? Why?

Son

ANGEL OF DEATH
MAN IN BLACK

Can't move his feet or his hands
Limbs are strapped by tough steel bands
Screen of wire stretched across his chest
The lights go dim, the chair does the rest
As the condemned breathes a last breath
Who should he see but the angel of death
The angel flew in laughing just to say
Death don't come easy if you lived the wrong way
Ya' know! I gotcha now, it's too late to pray

Machine gun man just shooting along
Thinking with a gun he can't go wrong
Though one night while asleep in a shack
Slick slipped in and put a knife in his back
And ya' know, before his bones went slack
Who should enter but a big man in black
The giant stalked in wickedly just to say
Death don't come easy if you lived the wrong way

Father

DEATH AND BLACK

I saw the Angel of Death and the Man in Black
During the war by a railroad track
Death reached in his burlap sack
Handed a chain with a name to his pal Black
I raised my rifle scope to see the name
And a cold chill went through my veins
I felt a frozen moment in time
When I realized the name was mine
I dropped my gun
And started to run
A gun can't stop the Man in Black
Too late for a sniper to take it all back
With a little luck I got away that day
But the Man in Black is on his way

Son

THE DEVIL IS COMING

I am the Devil and I am coming after you
I know that you were expecting me too
What did you think your afterlife of
After giving hate and never no love

Did you ever once fill a person with cheer
Instead of always creating more fear
Don't beg to me, your pleas are in vain
You must suffer for your victims' pain

There is no amendment you didn't break
Now it is thy soul that I shall take
To the place of everlasting night
Where you will remain in eternal fright

In the sinners' fiery place called Hell
Is where your misfortunate soul will dwell
In my black book your name is signed
Never again any peace shall ye find

Father

DEVIL'S WALKING STICK

I met the Devil and he had a goatee
And he knew the Bible better than me
He said Jesus was his best friend
But it was lies and false hope in the end
Hope I never see that bastard again

I'd be a fool to grab the Devil's walking stick
But I got a .45 that would cut him to the quick
If we ever meet on a dark lonely street
I fear for him and for me
Because the last thing I want...
Is to become He

Son

THE GODS RELAX

Burning castles light the sky with a lavender flame
Crying clouds spill silver tears without shame
Sighing trees sit patiently with wooden hearts in pain
Laughing children hope that life is just a game
Long-haired hippies search desperately for a vein
Lovely ladies watch sin get sucked down a dirty drain
And the Gods relax, knowing the Earth is in vain

Munching beetles clamp strong jaws in stalks of sugar cane
Growling dogs break tough necks to break a steel chain
Shaggy lions watch fleet gazelles and shake a tawny mane
Galloping cancer rides in search of a nicotine stain
And me, I just lean out on the window pane
See that nothing, nowhere is quite the same
And the Gods relax, knowing the Earth is in vain

Father

ONE DARK AND RAINY NIGHT

One dark and rainy night
God summoned my spirit
And dropped me on the floor
Right in the middle of a spiritual war
I woke up in an unfamiliar room
In the presence of four beasts of doom
Two by the stairs, one above me, and one by the door
Dark, heartless shadows that could change their form
Paralyzed with fear, I've never been so scared
Until a beast took my wife and kids up the stairs
Then I knew that this was war

I fought like hell with anger and rage
With the heart of a lion, but trapped in a cage
As the smoky beasts were winning the fight
God stepped in and gave me his light
I killed three beasts and climbed the stairs
And when I finally killed the fourth
My will and spirit could take no more
Godspeed, I was back on Earth
Knowing more of what life is worth
Many times I thought the Earth was in vain
Many times I blamed God for my pain
But on that dark and rainy night
God summoned my spirit and set me right

Son

SUICIDE

If you do cheat
Hey! Take it slow
Don't let me go
On down the hill
Oh, tell me lover
Is it all over
Oh, tell me lover
Is there another
Don't wait until
I have jumped
Jumped off the hill

Father

DARK WORD

There's a certain word
I've heard many use
A word of darkness
A word of gloom
We've all heard of it
When spoken
It hovers thick in the air
A black cloud
Like one before a storm
Sometimes it rains
But lightning seldom strikes
'Cause it's a word for the selfish
For the weak
Most are all talk
Pity they want
They thrive on your guilt
They don't know the effects
And the pain of others
They don't care
This word is a curse
A mental weapon
From this guilt trip you cannot hide
This word, it tortures
This word is...
Suicide

Son

FRUSTRATION MAN

Hey frustration! Why are you here?
Get off my back, outta my mind
Cause I ain't gonna take no more
I got a gun for things unkind
And just to make it real clear
Let's shoot it out, frustration man

Hey frustration! Why are you back?
Irritating me with a nasty nudge
Get outta me, go on outta sight
Explosion is bursting in my soul
I'm ready for you with dynamite
Against irony I hold a grudge
Gonna bomb you out, frustration man

Hey frustration! Who invited you?
I didn't ask for no bad news
Don't try to crash my party
By now I paid all my dues
Oh, let me go! Let me live
My only weapon is suicide
I ain't talking no jive, frustration man

Father

CAN'T SURRENDER

Bleeding from life's wounds
Fighting the pain
Can't give up
Or the beast will reign
The fire is tempting
Pressure seems never ending
Looking for sunshine
All I see is a greyish haze
And death looks easier every day

The storm is thrashing in the dark of the night
I can't surrender
The sky is infinite black
Lightning sheds the only light
I can't surrender
Like a candle caught in the rain
Searching for light, an eternal flame
I won't surrender

Society has crushed my deepest pride
I'll revenge their insults
And the Devil won't get me
'Til I've finished my ride
Living in the shadows
A land of darkness and violence
Can't give in
Gotta hold my faith
And listen…
For the music in the silence

Son

LIFETIME PAIN

I once had a wound that hurt and bled
I once was hungry and without bread
I once was tired and there was no bed
I once was sad and wished I was dead

Who cares if it is a tough sad game
Who cares if a blind man has no cane
Who cares if a baby cries in vain
I care…but it's just lifetime pain

Father

DON'T WANT TO BE DEAD

If I had no head
I would be dead
I'd have no pain
No sorrow
No worries
No cares
I would also have
No thoughts
No love
No emotions
No life
I'll keep my head
Don't want to be dead

Son

LIVE TO DIE

I gotta crash someday
There can be no other way
It may be by way of age
I doubt it on a stage
Someday I must lay on down
Give my body back to earth
Live to die is all I found
Nothing is all it ends up worth
Maybe soon I just may die
Insurance prices are so high
My wife may pray or cry
I think I will miss her much
Yes, someday I gotta go
Yet it won't be on the moon
Might be desert sands or snow
It may be far away or soon
One day I will be real cold
Lose my life on a silver plane
Man so young, hope I'm old
When I get the dying pain
I gotta see it to the end
There can be no other way

Father

SO WE PRAY

Life to me seems so strange
Like I'll never understand it
Yet I live it every day
Live to die to live again
Or so they say
And so we pray…
But just the other day
I almost cried
For a girl I never knew
I met her friends the day after she died
I believe she's in a better place
Yet it seems so strange
Because I still cried

Son

THE FALL OF A LEAF*

I am a leaf
Burdened by grief
It is the coming of fall
No hope of life within me at all
And when the time has come to be
I will be twisted off my tree
I hear my mates and friends cry
It is a sad thing to die
A cruel touch of nature's hand
Taking us from our branching land
Oh, I feel the cold winds blow
So easily, my greenness did go
I hear the trees growl
Ah, the pain!…torn from bough
Thinking, as I fall below
It is time to die I know
I miss the security of the tree
Oh, loneliness embeds within me
Being whipped and tossed around
Upon the coldness of the ground
I feel my strength is going
Gee, how ragged I am showing
As I die, I hope my son
Will not see what is done
Me now, later my son

Father

* The fall was Pat's favorite time of year. He was born in the
fall, and sadly, he died in the fall. The original version of this
poem did not include the last line. He added it shortly before his
death. Ironically, Pat's son Ryan died six months after he did.

166

SOME YOUNG TREE

Stand alone
Looking up
At my favorite maple tree
Still to be here
Years before, and years after me
Childhood memories dance around this tree
The shelter it gives
Costs no admission; it's free!

I hope someday
When the lumberjacks carry me away
That they bury me
Underneath some young tree
So I can sacrifice my body
And pay my respects
To my favorite race and breed
The tree

Son

JESUS WHISPERED*

Went to catch a train
While walking on my way
A whisper seemed to say
"Believe in me my friend"
I thought it just imagination
As I tarried to the station
Alone, I glanced around
No other was to be found
In the cry of the wind
I heard the words again
"Believe in me my friend"
"Who?" I cried out loud
Jesus showed his face and smiled
Since the whisper of that day
Life has really been okay
He walks beside me every day
Yes, life has really been okay

Father

* I believe this is the last poem Pat wrote. Pat usually wrote at night. He always woke me up to show me any new poems he wrote. I never saw this one. When I opened the suitcase where he kept his poetry to find a suitable one to be read at his funeral, this poem was on top of all the others. It looked freshly written as the paper had no wrinkles or smudges. I believe this is a true testimony of his personal relationship with Jesus Christ.

THIS MAN

This man you speak of
I have not yet met
But I believe
He will accept me in His net
This man you speak of
I pray to befriend
And walk beside Him
Through the sand
I want to hold the hand
That touches yours
I need Him
To pull my soul ashore
This man you speak of
Please tell him I'm here
Ask Him to forgive
My doubts and fear
Tell Him I would love to say
"Life has really been okay!"

Son

Patrick J. O'Shea (father) was born in Salem, Ohio on October 31, 1951. He soon moved to western Pennsylvania, where he lived for the remainder of his life. He married his high school sweetheart, Carolyn Everett, and they had two children. He was a railroad conductor working out of Conway Yards, Pennsylvania, but poetry was his true passion. *Conversations We Never Had* is a collection debuting some of his best writing. Pat's hobbies included drawing, fishing, and playing basketball.

Patrick J. O'Shea (son) was born in New Brighton, Pennsylvania on November 12, 1970. He currently lives near Philadelphia with his wife and two children. He is a musician, a teacher, and a writer. He has written articles for music magazines and for outdoors publications. The book *Conversations We Never Had* is his debut as an author/poet. Patrick has a love for the outdoors and spends his free time hiking, hunting, fishing, and shooting traditional archery.

Here are a few pictures from the short time
we had together in this life.

Made in the USA
Middletown, DE
09 July 2022

68916573R00106